# cries of a warrior

*a poetic journey through cultivating revival*

# morgan fuller

copyright 2018

ISBN: 9780692083543

# Foreword

Morgan Fuller has written one of the best prophetic poetry books we have ever read. Cries of a Warrior will challenge you and inspire you to go after God with all your heart. These poems are prophetic declarations full of power that will enhance your prayer life. Morgan's words will ring true with every intercessor and prayer warrior. Morgan's heart for personal revival is so evident in every poem.

We have loved hearing these poetic war cries for years, and we are excited that Morgan is now sharing this message with the world. The Dawson's are so proud of Morgan and her willingness to use her gift to the fullest. This would make an excellent gift for anyone, so order numerous copies and give them out!

Joe Joe & Autumn Dawson
Founder of Roar Apostolic Network &
Author of Kingdom Mindset

# Introduction

It is almost surreal sitting here writing this introduction to a book I've carried for so long. How do I even begin? In dry seasons and abundant seasons, I have carried these poems in my spirit knowing God must have a purpose for them. It is a humbling thing being entrusted to carry something for The Lord.

The Lord has used these poems and the experiences that brought them forth to shape my life, character, and integrity in so many ways. To make me into the person I was created by Him to be. He has used some of them to heal broken places inside of me. He has used them to burden my heart for the church to be what He has called them to. God has even used them to remind me in times that I could not feel His presence that He has never left me. Be assured, my friend, He has never left you either. He never will.

As I have written each one, The Lord has given my voice back. He has emboldened me to speak His truth with authority and power. It is my hope that by sharing them with you, God will use these poems in some way to restore your voice as well.

These pages are filled with some of the most intimate parts of my journey so far with The Lord. I've shared with you moments of failure, refreshing, grieving, and desperation. I've shared challenging moments, the joy of God's presence, the solitude of bondage, and moments of freedom through God's deliverance. This mantling process, this becoming a warrior, has been no easy task. He is still making me the warrior He has called me to be. The warfare has been strong but His peace is stronger. It's been challenging but it has also been more fulfilling than I would have ever imagined. God's process will always produce the best you.

Friend, I beg of you, do not despise your process. He is growing you into something beautiful and mighty for His Kingdom. You are valuable and you have so much purpose inside of you just waiting to burst forth. Find your God-given voice and open your mouth! Heaven is backing you! The Earth is waiting for you to live what God has called you to. Pick up your mantle and run! Be encouraged and live wild! Isn't it time your voice is heard?

# Contents

Broken Beauty ..................................................................10
Miracle Worker ................................................................12
What You See ..................................................................14
Devotion ..........................................................................16
A Call To Arms ................................................................18
Overwhelmed Not Overcome ......................................20
Be The Standard ............................................................24
A Letter To My Enemy ..................................................26
Even So ............................................................................28
Be Strong and Courageous ..........................................30
I Prayed For You ............................................................32
The Physician Is In ........................................................34
Wild and Free ..................................................................38
The Greatest Thing I Will Ever Be ..............................40
In The Presence ..............................................................42
Give Myself Away ..........................................................46
Let It Start In Us .............................................................48
All And Only For Jesus .................................................50
Every Praise .....................................................................52
Prepare The Way ............................................................54
Ever Praise The Lord ....................................................56
Let Me Burn ....................................................................58
Carry Me A While ..........................................................62
Faithful Promises ...........................................................64
Battle Cry .........................................................................66
Forged By Fire ................................................................68
For That There Is Grace ...............................................70
Weight of Your Words ..................................................72
Love Isn't Pretty .............................................................74

# Broken Beauty

She is broken but she's beautiful
And she doesn't even know it
A holy vessel deceived by the enemy's lies
Hiding behind a mask and secretly she's no longer hopeful

Seeking love and approval in all the wrong places
With a made up face and skin tight dresses
She has a God sized hole
She's trying to fill with the world

She needs an Acts 9 revelation
A black and white moment
When she comes to the realization
She's a true daughter of The King
Not an imitation
Sitting on the back row

Trying to blend into a crowd that's different
Only here because someone insisted
Preacher blasts words that break the stone
And finally she knows that she isn't alone

All but running to the alter
She's desperate for change
A stirring in her heart
And God marks her forever

Blessed and redeemed
Bought at a price
Now highly esteemed
And joint heir with Christ

She has to share this new found love
Only turning back to reach those where she once stood
Knowing her past is not her prison
But a testimony of the One Person that can make a difference
Of true love and perfection

Peace at last
No need to impress
Because in the presence of Jesus
Her soul can finally rest.

# Miracle Worker

Religion would have you believe
That tradition and rules is Christian living
But our God is not a mannequin
Stiff and motionless
And He does not perform miracles for one generation while neglecting the next

Jesus still lives
Holy Spirit still speaks
And God still moves mountains
He moves in and through you.
Miracles happen when His children step out in faith

Within you He has placed power and authority
To tread on serpents
To call forth healing
And to cast out devils

Miracles rest in your hands
And deliverance waits to be spoken from your lips

The Father wants to use you

On the earth

In this hour!
To set the captives free
To lift up the fallen
And to heal the broken


Live in obedience and see miracles happen
It isn't your name on the line
It's His
Don't worry about the outcome
Or if they will be healed
Between me and you
Our God always comes through


All that depends on you
Is committing to be His hands and feet
A willing vessel
A light-bearer
Obedience to the calling of The Miracle Maker
Asking you to be a miracle worker

# What You See

You see me perfectly

Not perfectly in my imperfection

But as I will be

Perfected

You see who I will be

Your love is what grows me

Grows me to perfection that You already know

You see me beautiful

Glowing and pure

Not before you clean me up

But sparkling and new

According to Your perfect design

To You I am already a reflection of Your glory

Salvation creates a perfect bride before You

Spotless and without blemish

I am speechless

What can I say of the revelation of Your love for me?

You really do adore me

Completely

And unashamedly

You really see perfection when You gaze upon me

How can I comprehend this truth?

My human mind is not enough to understand

You love me

You see me

You call me perfect

Spotless

Beautiful

In Your eyes

No imperfection remains in me.

How can it be?

Show me what You see.

# Devotion

I will lift up a praise to the God who paid my pardon
The God who bought me and adopted me
The God who gave me a right to His promise

I will lift up a praise to the God who loved me lost in my sin
The God who sought me out in the midst of rebellion
The God who awakened me from death and gave me robes for grave clothes

You are the God who loves
The God who sees
The God who won the victory for me

Jesus, You have my whole heart
Where else would I go?
There is no god like You.

You laid your life down
Died a sinner's death
And by rising again
You paid the price so I might live

I won't let a single day be wasted
Not one word be idle

My desire is to enter into Your gates
Having used all You gave me
Completely spent of all You would grace to me for Your glory

Let no one leave my company question that I am bond-servant
only to You,
My King and Redeemer

I will praise You all my days.
Lift my voice to The King of Glory
Dance before the Lover of my soul
Worship at the feet of the Creator of All

Let my life be continual worship
Whole-hearted devotion
A reflection of Your love
Your hands and feet to a generation

Let them see You in me

# A Call To Arms

Revival is coming
It's time to suit up
Put on your armor
There's no time for sleeping
Stand at the ready, Christian
This is the time
Get up
Go out
The harvest is waiting
Our enemy is already moving
But God has equipped you
Don't be caught unaware
There's a people that need you
They don't know He's won their freedom
You have to tell them
You have to fight for them
Sickness and sin fill our city
But we have a good report
This land belongs to The King Of Heaven
Did you forget?
Wake up, Christian!
Souls are lost and dying

Do you not know?
God chose you for a war
Not to keep a pew warm!
You are a part of the remnant
A child of Zion
A carrier of light
A mighty warrior
And a hungry wild fire
Remember what you're called to!
Souls are waiting
There is no time to lose
Revival is coming
You can't just sit down
No!
You can't wait!
People are crying out
How long will you sleep through their screaming?
The devourer is near
Don't leave them to perish
There are many in bondage
And you have the key
You've been given authority
Break off their shackles by the power within you
Fight for them
Do not fear the enemy
He is defeated
Men of valor,
Women of grace,
Your time is now!
Revival is here!

# Overwhelmed Not Overcome

When my heart is overwhelmed
And sadness comes
I will say The Lord is good
When oceans rage
And storms surround me
I will say The Lord is my protector
He raises me up
And plants me in heavenly places
Despair has no hold
Circumstances have no authority
My God makes lasting decrees
He orders my steps and destiny
I will not fear
I will not worry

Though tears flow from my eyes
They sing a melody of hope and faith
Of trust in The King of All
My shield and defender
Comforter and friend
I find joy when I lay myself at His feet
There is freedom in His presence
It melts away cares of this world
Though my situation doesn't look like my promise
I know He has not forsaken me
The only Faithful One
Will complete His good work
I am not abandoned
No matter the lies of my enemy
I will rejoice and be glad
The victory is won
My God has restored me
The Lord has raised me to life again
My soul refreshed and my heart is at peace
There is nothing too great for Him
Who cares for me
I will ever praise The Lord

## Be The Standard

When the enemy comes in like a flood
God raises up a standard
Are you aware that you
A child of The King
You are that standard

Your prayers
Your warfare
Your declarations
And your decrees
By the power of Jesus Christ
And the authority of Holy Spirit within you

You are highly favored daughters
Not weaker
Not less
You are not easily beaten
Nor are you defeated
But victorious warriors
Taking their place in the fight against Hell
And the enemy of our souls

Mothers
You have a directive
Instructions straight from The Throne Room
Stand up and war for your children
For the next generation
Fight for their destiny
Their words of promise
Their lives
Fight for their very souls

Lead them in the way of everlasting life
Teach them to pursue God's presence
Show them what it means to war for the things of God to be made manifest in the earth

Young women
You are not without orders
Go and shift the atmospheres in your schools
Carry the glory of The Lord to your workplace
Display character and integrity in all you do
Overtake darkness
With the light that resides inside of you

Daughters of The Most High
We are not without purpose
Or without equal strength in this battle
God equips women to war alongside men
Intimate allies in the army of Heaven
Fighting side by side
Lifting them up
Covering their blindside

Linked arm in arm
A force empowered through Christ
To take the land for His Kingdom

Woman of God
Now is your time
Take your place
Open your mouth
Use your God given voice

Daughters
Warriors
It is time that we rise up
And Be The Standard

# A Letter To My Enemy

I refuse to be distracted
Side tracked by your ploy
Enemy of my soul
I'm not falling for your tricks anymore

I know this attack is to hinder me
But The One who created me already prepared my way

Jesus warned me you would come
That you would try to destroy me
But my God says I am more than a conqueror
That I have authority over you
Because I am His daughter

Do you know what His children have that you don't, Lucifer?
We have God's ear
His hand
But most importantly
His heart

His love for us is a hedge of protection
It is our victory shout
His love for us is a strong tower
Where we find refuge
And it is a mighty sword
Wielded against you for even thinking
That you would harm His beloved

I have something to tell you, Devil
I will not let you intimidate me any longer
I know in Whom I believe
I know Whose I am

My feet are planted on solid ground
And my roots have grown deep in Him
I will not be shaken
The God of all holds me secure

I rebuke you
I command you to loose my family and let them go
You have no place among the children of God
In Jesus Name

Satan,
Jesus has defeated you!
You are under His feet.

## Even So

Your word says grief only lasts for the night

But how long is this night season?

I'm ready for the joy that comes with the morning

A bit overwhelmed with sorrows like water

Crashing over me like a wave

And I can't breathe

I can't breathe

Mouth to mouth

Pumping my chest

Willing my heart to beat and my lungs to

BREATHE

Oh Lifeguard of my life

I hold to truth

I trust you are good

And you tread upon the waves pulling me under

Though the hurricane rages

You hold me secure

Pour life into this frame

In weakness and despair

I won't be left to drown

Lifted by Your mighty hand

Grief will pass

Then joy comes

In it all

I am never alone

If this night must last a while longer

Even so,

You are still good

# Be Strong and Courageous

Be strong and courageous
I am giving you your mountain
Do not be afraid
I am slaying the giants

Be strong and courageous
I am with you in the battle
Do not be afraid
I am the fire of your torches and the sounding of your trumpets

Be strong and courageous
I will see you through
Do not be afraid
I will protect you on every side

Be strong and courageous
I have already made a way
Do not be afraid
I have won your victory

Be strong and courageous
I will not let you be overcome
Do not be afraid
I will not let your enemy gloat over you

Be strong and courageous
I have set a table before you in the presence of your enemies
Do not be afraid
I have anointed your head with oil

Be strong and courageous
Do not be afraid
I am your God
I know you by name

Be strong and courageous
Do not be afraid
You are secure in Me
And I never fail

# I Prayed For You

I prayed for you today
Not just in passing thought
Fervently, I cried out
For your future
Your life
Your soul

I prayed for you today
For you to hear His voice
That you would encounter The Lord

I prayed for you today
That your heart would be soft
And your spirit brave

I prayed for you today
For healing and for wholeness
That chains of bondage be broken
And strongholds torn down

I prayed for you today
That you wouldn't give up on yourself
Or lose hope

I prayed for you today
Made war against the plans of the enemy
If he wants you
He will have to pry you from my prayers

I prayed for you today
For salvation and redemption
Your purpose
Your destiny
Your God-given dreams

I prayed for you today
That you wouldn't feel alone
Or abandoned

I prayed for you today
And I'll pray for you tomorrow

# The Physician Is In

Numb

Just like novocaine

But it wears off

Just a band aid

Not getting to the root of the pain

We'd rather cover it up

Don't want to deal with it

We want to hide instead

But our God is better than that

He wants more for you

A divine healing

That's what is waiting

Waiting at His office door

Let's step into the exam room

Don't worry

Do not fear
Allow The Lord to heal your wounds
You won't let the tears fall
Suck it up
Carry on
No one will notice that broken limb you are limping on
Don't you know?
That's how infection starts
God sees that injury
And He has a remedy
Cast aside temporary relief
Receive wholeness with simple belief
All it takes is the smallest mustard seed
Don't you want to be free of this affliction?
You have a divine appointment
Come consult The Healer
The Great Physician is in
And He is here to meet your need

# Wild and Free

Broken
Rusty
Discarded

My life a mess
And my mind chaotic
I saw no value in me

I had done too much
Missed the mark
My heart in disarray
Who would ever see something good in me?

Scars left behind from punishing myself
I deserved it
Bruising to match the beaten places within me

Unloved

Unwanted

Undone

Shattered glass on the floor

From the broken windows of my soul

Letting whispers of the disappointment I was sweep in on the wind

Rusty tin attempting to hide the pain of a broken life

All the while I hid

Ashamed of the depth of my sin

Who had I become?

What kind of life was this?

Surely this was not living

A captive

Isolated

Alone in my prison

Fear was the warden

And shame was my guard

Would I ever be free?

Would torment always be my portion?

Deafening silence broke my heart
Solitary confinement that fractured my spirit

Alone
Trapped
Splintered

Can anyone hear me?

Then,
Through the silence I heard a voice
Calling out
"Child, I've always been here."
And with just a breath
My prison doors opened wide

Music filled my soul
And joy overcame depression

Strong hands took mine in His
And I danced for the first time

My heart of stone
Exchanged for one of flesh
Scars and bruises
Replaced with a message of hope

Grave clothes became Robes of righteousness
He placed a ring upon my hand
And a crown upon my head

Jesus came
And He wanted me

No longer broken and undone
But useful in His kingdom
Valued by The King

Sweet Savior
Cleaned me up and gave me a home
Released me from the shackles
He made me new

I once was a prisoner
Bound and nearly dead

But now I live
Wild and Free

# The Greatest Thing I Will Ever Be

I could never dance with enough grace to portray Your beauty
But I can dance for the pleasure of Your Presence

I could never sing in such a key to reflect Your majesty
But I can sing of Your many blessings all my days

I could never write enough words to explain Your deity
But I can pour out my heart with every syllable

I could never speak with enough eloquence to be worthy of speaking Your Name

But I can tell of Your great love with endless gratitude

I could never tell of the depth of Your abounding mercy
But I can shout of the miraculous things You have done for me

I could never know every facet of You
But I can commune with you for my whole life

I could never say enough thank yous for Your sacrifice
But I can worship You with every breath

With all I could never do
You love me still

With all I could never say
You choose me still

I am unworthy but you call me righteous

In all my life the greatest thing I could never be
But grace declares I am
Is Yours

# In The Presence

Bonds are broken
Shackles cast off
Dancing in the presence
That melts my mountains

Love overflows
It covers me
Cleanses every spot
And makes me whole

Let prayer be my covering
And peace surround me
Resting in heavenly places
Here worries cannot reach me

Joy unspeakable
Laughter pours out
Depression cannot linger
Sadness is nowhere about

Hear my praise, O Lord
Sing over Your daughter
I have come to worship You
In spirit and in truth

Cleanse the most inward places
Burn away the impurities
Let my life be a constant sacrifice
Pure, Holy, and Righteous

Because of Your goodness, God
Faith does flourish
Your promises are true
And Your love never fails

I will worship You
For all my days
My hunger for more of You
Will never be satisfied

I thirst for the living water
For Your presence every hour
Meet with me, Lord
Let me dwell in Your house forever

# Give Myself Away

As a little girl I was always eager to please

I did all I could to make people happy

To go above and beyond

Thinking it would put my mind at ease

If I just got good grades

If I could run that mile

So I gave myself away

And I poured it into what I thought would bring my daddy home

What I thought would make him proud of me

As a teen in high school

I learned to dress a certain way

And walk the walk that would make me cool

Filling my mind with the latest garbage on the radio and reality TV

I just hoped someone would see me

So I gave myself away
And forgot who I wanted to be
I forgot what I liked
And hid what wasn't "in" about me

As a young woman trying to find my way
I noticed a void inside my chest that stole the breath from me
So I gave myself away
To men who would trade affections for what they wanted from me
I gave myself away to working a dead end job so I could say
"I am making my own way"
I gave myself to every lust of sinful flesh
Hoping to fill that painfully empty place

But one day a friend
A real friend
Was brave enough to introduce me to a God who loves me
The God who takes delight in me

I met Jesus

Who healed my heart

And made me whole

Jesus

Who restored every piece I had thrown away

I met Jesus

The Word made flesh

Who gave Himself away

For me

Now every day I give myself away

I crucify that sinful flesh

To live the life I was created to

And be who I should have been all along

A blessed and highly favored

Daughter of the True King

Declaring His truth to the nations

Pouring His love on those who give themselves away

Just like me

Lost and undone

I give myself away

For His glory

And His kingdom

Because I have found something greater than me

I have found Who was missing

And Who filled that awful emptiness

I give myself away

Because The King gave himself away

For me

# Let It Start In Us

I am not content to sit by the side
While those in this world die
What right do I have to be silent
When I carry the light of life?
Lord, Here am I
Send me
I will be the one
Standing at the edge of this city
Declaring
"Come back to God!"
I will go
If they perish
Let it be over the cries of my heart
It they walk themselves into hell
Let it be with me desperately fighting for their souls
How could one so willingly let the lost and undone

Walk by without hearing His name?
Without sharing His good news?
Jesus gave himself away
To make them new
Just like He did for you
Christian!
Stand up with me
Don't let them go unaware
Do not sit quietly
Declare the word of The Lord
Urge them
"Come back to God!"
Shout to this city
"Come back to God!"
Here we are Lord
Send us!
We will usher in revival
But Lord,
Let Revival start with us!

# All And Only For Jesus

I incline my ear
Because Your voice casts out fears

I give my heart
Because Your hand can heal its parts

I turn my eyes to The One who saves

I lift my hands
To You who makes me free

I lay down my crown
Before The One upon the throne

I give my life to The One who created it

I submit my steps
Because You are the one who makes my path straight

I lift my voice
Because only You, Jesus, are worthy of praise

Only You are worthy
Only You are holy
Only You can save
Only You can redeem
Only You make new, Jesus, Only You

I am Yours
I give my life to serve You

My hands
My feet
My voice
My heart
All tools for Your kingdom

Use me, Lord
My soul longs to bless You
Only You, Jesus

# Every Praise

Stumbling in the dark
Blinded
Unseeing
In need of a light
Stretching forward
Trying to feel my way
Hindered by the black
Can anybody find me?

Then I heard Him
"Child" He Thundered
"Come forth"
Light illuminated the world around me

There it was
My way of escape
I burst through the open grave
Into the arms of Jesus
My Jesus
The Living Jesus

Rescued
And now I'm free
Under the shadow of His wings

I dance in new liberty
What have I to offer but extravagant praise?

So I will pour out my life
To Jesus
The Life Giver

All that I own could never be enough to thank Him
All that I could say would never express the wonder of my heart

You are worthy of so much more than I could ever offer
But I'll give my all to dwell in Your presence all of my days
Mighty Warrior of Heaven

You are worthy of everything I can give
So I'll pour myself out
Pour myself out
POUR MYSELF OUT
To give You
My Jesus
Every praise

Stand up every Christian
Has He not rescued you?
Wake up
Come back to life
Be revived
and pour yourselves out
Pour yourselves out
POUR YOURSELVES OUT

Our Jesus deserves every praise

# Prepare The Way

Dreamers
It is time to awaken
There is work to be done
Those dreams are not for your entertainment
They are divine instructions, warnings, and confirmations
Straight from the throne room of Heaven
Do not sit on the dreams God has given you
He is calling you to take action

World Changers
You have been set apart and appointed
Born for just this moment
To be a voice in the desert
A river in dry places
You were made to shift atmospheres
Created to carry the spirit of freedom
To shake prison doors
And tear down strongholds
Created to break chains

Warriors
Gather your weapons
And put on your armor
God has set you on a battlefield
To be His instrument of war

Have no fear
No weapon formed will prosper
No enemy attack will prevail
Draw your sword
Ready your shield
Fight from the position of victory
For your King is the victor

Intercessors
Contend more fervently than before
Enter His courts with thanksgiving
Petition your righteous King
Declare life over your region
Take authority over powers and principalities
This is your calling
To be a covering
Destined to turn the spiritual tide of your time

Children of God
Do not grow weary
This is your moment
Rise up, Beloved of Christ
Your hour has come
Keep the fire burning
Your mind renewed
And your sword at the ready
Storm the enemy's camp
Lift a shout to shake his gates
The King is coming
All you His people
Take your place
Prepare the way

# Ever Praise The Lord

When my heart is overwhelmed
And sadness comes
I will say The Lord is good

When oceans rage
And storms surround me
I will say The Lord is my protector

He raises me up
And plants me in heavenly places
Despair has no hold
Circumstances have no authority

My God makes lasting decrees
And He orders my steps and destiny

I will not fear
I will not worry

Though tears flow from my eyes
They sing a melody of hope and faith

Trust in the King of All
My Shield and Defender
Comforter and Friend

I find joy when I lay myself at His feet
There is freedom in His presence
It melts away the cares of this world

Though my situation doesn't look like my promise
I know He has not forsaken me
The only Faithful One
Will complete His good work

I am not abandoned
No matter the lies of my enemy
I will rejoice and be glad
The victory is won

My God has restored me
The Lord has raised me to life again
My soul refreshed and my heart is at peace

There is nothing too great for Him who cares for me
I will ever praise The Lord

# *Let Me Burn*

Burn away this complacency

Stagnant waters I'm dwelling in

Stir me up

I won't settle for a flicker of light

Make me a wildfire

A living sacrifice

May the scent of my worship please you

A pretty service for a Sunday masquerade

It just won't do

My weaknesses hidden in a vault

I open the door for You to rush in

Burn me clean

Sick and tired of the screen play

This scripted dialogue is exhausting

Father

You are about behind the scenes

Let's get down to the business of restoring me

I don't care how ugly

Remove the mire

I give You the ash

Lord

I pour myself out

Create in me a heart that's alive

I desire to be a burning one

The light and warmth that all can feel and see

Genuine fire that sparks a revolution

A catalyst for change

Contagious and furious

Uncontainable

Lord

Let me burn

# Carry Me A While

Lord, I am weary

I'm unsure I can even lift my head

But You are already aware

And You are ready to meet me here

When I feel like giving up

And love seems so far from me

You sing a sweet melody

Help my ears to hear

And my heart to receive

Lord, I'm lonely

And I don't know how to pray

This longing

This groaning

I miss Your presence

Can I ever come back from this?

Can I be set free for good?

How can my heart grow so cold?

You've placed everything in my hands

Voluntarily I've given it back

I let rebellion consume me

Earthly desires overtake me again

You created me

So only You can fix me

Fix me!

Uproot the evil within me

Expose every wrong

My God

Take this from me

I do what I don't want to do

And I don't do what I wish to do

This flesh is tearing at my soul

Burn it away

Let it be a sacrifice on Your altar

My heart breaks at the sin I can't shake

I'm in a desperate place

Lord, make a change in me!

I can't bear to live this way

Free Me!

Lord, don't allow me to be separated from You!

Keep me close

Refresh me!

Renew me!

Lord, I'm tired and weary

Won't you carry me a while?

Your eyes never wander

And Your love has never wavered

Though I run and hide

You still seek me out

Turn my heart back to You once more

Carry me a while

Let Your words be refreshing to my spirit

Surround me O Lord

Capture my heart again

Set me back on the narrow path

But hold my hand

Don't let me fall

Be ever present

Keep me, Lord

And when I grow weak and faint

Carry me a while more

# Faithful Promises

When doubt creeps in
I know You keep Your promises
Thoughts whisper
That's not what you heard
That's not what He said
NO!
You are faithful to Your promises
And You are for me
You have a plan for my life
To prosper me
And not to harm me
A gift and a calling that is irrevocable
You are faithful to keep Your promises
I remind myself
I stir up my spirit
I know You love me

Like the crashing waves of the sea
So, Your love crashes over me
When I reach for You
Your love surrounds me
Like the depths of the ocean
The water of Your word washes me clean
And I am overcome by Your glory
How can I not worship?
How can I not declare the works of Your hand?
You are beautiful
Your love is fierce
And Your promises are true
Your thoughts for me outnumber the sand
You have called me
And destined me for divine purpose
You will not delay when I cry out
You re my ever present help
When I need reminding
I tell myself
You are a covenant God
You are faithful to your promises
And Your promises are for me

# Battle Cry

Quiet steps
One foot in front of the other
My body is tired
My spirit is leaping
Into the upper room
Securing the door
This time belongs to The Lord
His presence engulfs me
"Speak Lord"
My heart's request
Like a soldier waiting for orders
Who can I love today?
Where is He leading?
Prostrate on the floor
Desperately contending
My weapons of warfare
Prayer
Petition
Holy Ghost fire burning
Early in the morning

Late into the night
The Lord calls for intercession
Warrior in the secret place
Don't let your soul grow weary
Now is your time
Push through
Basic training has ended
War is upon you
The battlefield is before you
Lift up a shout
Praise is your banner and your sword
Prayer is your covering and your axe
Raise your voice
Let a battle cry roar from deep within
War torn prayers and desperate fighting
The world won't go without climbing over you
Stand up
Take your position
Blow the shofar
Run in victory
And take back what was stolen
This land and these people are The Lord's
Don't give way and do not sit down
He has clearly spoken
Rising to my feet with a tear streaked face
I am ready to face the day
I can go with assurance because I know
My adversary is defeated
And my God has heard my battle cry

# Forged By Fire

When life seems hard
And the battle rages
When your courage wears thin
And the load gets heavy
You are being forged by fire

When you're struggling
Can't seem to catch a breathe
Keep pressing
When the enemy is whispering in your ear
That you are all alone and no one cares
Rebuke that
You are being forged by fire

When you can't see which way to go
And everything seems so dark
Remember where your light comes from
When you feel lost
And can't find your way

Remember who it is that guides you
You are being forged by fire

You are not blind and unarmed
You have been equipped
You have been trained
Your sword has been tempered by war
A war for the freedom of your soul
Your blade has been balanced by the Master Craftsman
And your footing is sure
You have been forged by fire

Do not fear mighty warrior
though the war ahead looks daunting
And the load you carry seems too heavy
Do not tremble
Even if it looks like you must fight alone
You are never alone in the fire

This city needs you
You, who has come out of the wilderness
You, whose character has been proven in the midst of adversity
You, who fought the lion, the bear, and the giant
You, who had every reason to give up and give in but remained steadfast

This city needs a warrior like you
A warrior
Forged by fire

# For That There Is Grace

The daily struggle
That thought you have to take captive
A little slip
The crashing fall
Every unclean thing
God has made provision
In His plan is your redemption
The little foxes lay waste to your best intentions
Hidden places
The believed deceptions
Hurt feelings and grudges
Secret sins you can't seem to let go
There is hope of freedom
God's payment for your pardon
It's nothing short of miraculous
The things you don't think can be cleansed
His answer for you is grace
Being an unfaithful bride
He loves us still
And so hedges us up

In His divine protection
Shielding us from ourselves
And the other lovers we run to
Rebellion ridden souls
Bent on getting into trouble
He is not taken by surprise
But has already made a way
His response is unfailing love
And as we turn with our hearts set on repentance
He says
There is grace
Go and sin no more
You are pardoned
The price is paid
You are no longer a slave
But have been made free
Every morning when you wake
I will be sure to remind you
My grace covers all today holds
Go in peace
Walk in salvation
You don't have to fall
You don't have to fear
Face every situation and thought
From the place I have established you
From the position of victory
Tell these things that come against you
The accusations
The condemnation
No.
For that,
I have been given grace

# Weight of Your Words

Words
Just like The Father's
You create a frequency that ripples
Power sent out through all of time
Listen to this progression

A young boy
Chastised with a little more than disappointment in his father's voice
Grows up his whole life
Behaviors he doesn't know the cause
But he rips himself apart for all his flaws
A still small voice tells him he is loved
But he can't hear it for the one screaming he's not enough

Be careful what you say
It's going to grow
Are you planting faith?
Are you depositing love?
What will you do with the power you possess?
Will you speak life
Or pour out death?

A little girl
She hears mommy say she isn't thin enough
Watching mom beat her own self up
She grows up
Twisted thinking
A number on a scale defines her beauty
She can't hear The Father tell her He created her perfect
The images on the TV screen
Models in a magazine
Shouting "You aren't pretty"

Can we understand the weight of our words?
The power to speak and make a lasting effect
Are you planting faith?
Are you depositing love?
What will you do with the power you possess?
Will you speak life
Or pour out death?

An endless cycle of people beat down
With words that hold power we can never know
Be the one who changes the tide
Begin a cycle of life and light

Speak what builds up
Change the thinking of a generation
Build a future that's bright
Start a fire of revival

Speak life
Speak light
Pour out Jesus
Be Revival

# Love Isn't Pretty

Love isn't pretty

It's not sweet and easy

It isn't simple and effortless

Love isn't butterflies and flowers

Love is a racing heart and furrowed brow

It's nail pierced hands and a thorny crown

Love is sacrifice

It's purchased with the blood of our Savior

It's each stripe He bore

And every step up that hill

Love is each splinter scraping His tender broken body

It's the labored breathing of the Sacrificial Lamb

The despair of separation from The Father

Love is the bridge He built for each of us

Love is late nights and early mornings in the secret place

Love is contending in this spiritual warfare

Love is a heart set on obedience no matter the cost

Love is faithful submission to The One who laid it all down for us

Love is bloody

Messy

Beautiful

Painful

Glorious

Love is adventurous

Exciting

Heart Wrenching

Laborious

Undignified

Love is determination

Admiration

Selfless

Submissive

Generous

Love is a great many things

But love is nothing as simple as

Pretty

www.ingramcontent.com/pod-product-compliance
Lightning Source LLC
Chambersburg PA
CBHW072106290426
44110CB00014B/1851